THE LITANY OF
THE TREE OF LIFE

in the tradition of

The Druidical Order
of the Golden Dawn

John Michael Greer

AEON

First published in 2022 by
Aeon Books

British Library Cataloguing in Publication Data

A C.I.P. for this book is available from the British Library

ISBN-13: 978-1-91350-494-6

Typeset by Medlar Publishing Solutions Pvt Ltd, India
Printed in Great Britain

www.aeonbooks.co.uk

THE LITANY OF THE TREE OF LIFE

CONTENTS

FOREWORD

It was in 1995 that I first encountered a slim pamphlet by William G. Gray entitled *The Office of the Holy Tree of Life*. Published by a small occult press in Texas in 1970, it set out a litany for the Tree of Life using Gray's own distinctive Cabalistic correspondences. I was impressed both by the litany itself and by the broader project, central to much of Gray's later writing, of developing rituals for the contemplative and devotional side of magical spirituality. Other projects demanded my attention at the time, but some years later I worked with Gray's litanies extensively, along with the rest of his Sangreal Sodality rituals.

That took place while I was in the early stages of a far more ambitious project. In 2003, while studying the archives of the Order of Bards Ovates and Druids (OBOD) at the invitation of its Chosen Chief Philip Carr-Gomm, I discovered fragments of the rituals and practices of a defunct magical order that had combined the nature spirituality of the Druid Revival with the ceremonial magic of the Hermetic Order of the Golden Dawn. Over the next few years I found traces of several similar traditions, none of which appears to have survived intact. Since by then I was both a longtime Golden Dawn practitioner and an initiate of three different Druid traditions, the obvious solution was reverse-engineering a similar system from the same raw materials. I began systematic practice of the resulting system in 2008; in 2013 the core practices were published in my book *The Celtic Golden Dawn*; a small but active magical order, the Druidical Order of the Golden Dawn (DOGD), sprang up promptly thereafter.

Some of the members of that order expressed an interest in the contemplative and devotional side of the Druidical Cabala I had devised for that project, and I was more than ready to meet them halfway. While Gray's Holy Office of the Tree of Life was unsuitable for DOGD use, a parallel project using the distinctive symbolism and ceremonies of the DOGD in place of Gray's equivalents turned out to be very well suited indeed. The first draft of the book in your hands, the *Litany of the Tree of Life*, followed swiftly, and was circulated privately among members of the order. It was on its third revision when Aeon Books expressed an interest in bringing it out for a more general audience.

The Litany of the Tree of Life is a relatively simple ritual for contemplative, meditative, and devotional work with the Druidical Tree of Life. I have added an essay on the distinctive version of the Cabala used in the DOGD, so that no previous involvement with that system is needed to practice the Litany.

In closing, I would like to acknowledge Oliver Rathbone of Aeon Books, who took the lead in getting this and a good many of my other books into print; the members of the Druidical Order of the Golden Dawn for their enthusiasm, interest, and unfailingly helpful feedback; and especially the late William G. Gray, one of the most consistently original voices in twentieth-century occultism, for the inspiration that eventually led to this project. My thanks go with all.

THE DRUIDICAL CABALA

While the version of the Cabala most frequently encountered in modern Western magical lore has Jewish roots, the Cabala itself does not. In his magisterial work *On the Origins of the Cabala*, Gershom Scholem showed conclusively that the Tree of Life and other core elements of Jewish Cabalism were borrowed by medieval Jewish scholars and mystics from an older set of Gnostic traditions outside of Judaism. Scholem's insight, unpopular though it has been in some circles, is solidly backed up by the evidence; two slightly different versions of the Tree of Life are referenced by the second-century Pagan author Celsus and his third-century Christian critic Origen, for example, and a closely related diagram—the *Wu Chi T'u*—appears in Chinese neo-Confucian writings a century before the Tree of Life first appeared in Jewish mystical literature.

In discussing the Cabala, in other words, we are dealing with an ancient and widespread symbolic system that has taken on varying forms and been applied to many different religious, spiritual, and magical traditions. Its origins, as I hope to show in a future book, can be found in the Pythagorean movement of late Archaic Greece and its colonies, and all its varied forms—Jewish and Gentile, religious and magical, orthodox and wildly heretical—share core features with the teachings of the old Pythagoreans.

Whether anything like the Cabala found its way to the ancient Druids is an open question. In her book *The Druids*, Nora Chadwick makes a strong case for Pythagorean influence on the ancient Druids via the important Greek Pythagorean presence in southern Gaul, but what might or might not have been transmitted through those channels of influence is as unknowable today as the rest of the old Druid teachings. When the Druid Revival began to take shape in the eighteenth century, however, Pythagorean teachings quickly became part of the Revival tradition, and the Cabala followed in the early twentieth century as Golden Dawn initiates joined a variety of Druid Revival orders. Ross Nichols, the most influential twentieth-century Druid author, was among those who included the Cabala in his Druid teachings; his essay "Revised Cabala" (included along with other Cabalistic papers in Philip Carr-Gomm's *In the Grove of the Druids*) is one of several useful reworkings of the Tree from a Druid standpoint.

The Druidical Cabala used in this book, and in several other books I have written, uses ten Welsh titles of deity for the ten spheres of the Tree of Life, in place of the ten Hebrew titles used in many other versions of the Cabala. These are given in Table 1 below.

Table 1: The spheres of the Tree of Life

Number	Welsh name and meaning	Hebrew name and meaning
1	Celi, the Hidden	Kether, the Crown
2	Perydd, the Maker	Chokmah, Wisdom
3	Dofydd, the Tamer	Binah, Understanding
(unnumbered circle)	Iau, the Yoke	Daath, Knowledge
4	Ener, the Namer	Chesed, Mercy
5	Modur, the Mover	Geburah, Severity
6	Muner, the Lord	Tiphareth, Beauty
7	Byw, the Living	Netzach, Victory
8	Byth, the Eternal	Hod, Glory
9	Ner, the Mighty	Yesod, the Foundation
10	Naf, the Shaper	Malkuth, the Kingdom

The meaning of the ten spheres in the Druidical Cabala corresponds closely to equivalents in other Cabalistic systems, though the divine names and other religious symbolism is of course different, and an ecological symbolism is used in place of the astrological symbolism common in most Cabalistic systems—this is after all a Druid system. The symbols of the spheres also include geomantic figures (which are given their Welsh names here—see Table 4), Tarot cards, and letters of the Coelbren, the runelike magical alphabet of the Welsh bards. The symbolism used for the spheres in the Litany is shown in Table 2.

The twenty-two paths of the Tree of Life have a distinctive symbolism of their own, which includes Tarot cards, geomantic figures, and Coelbren letters, as shown below in Table 3.

Table 2: Symbolism of the ten spheres

Number	Divine name	Ecology	Geomancy	Tarot	Coelbren
1	OIW	Sun	Wholeness	4 Aces	(unknown)
2	Hu	Sun's Radiation	•	4 Fours	(unknown)
3	Ced	Sun's Gravity	• •	4 Eights	(unknown)
(none)	Ceridwen	Moon	(see diagram)	Court Cards	(unknown)
4	Belinus	Materials of Earth	(see diagram)	XXI, World	U
5	Taranis	Cycles of Time	(see diagram)	XX, Judgment	Y
6	Hesus	Life	Bendith Fawr	XIX, Sun	A
7	Elen	Plants	Colled	XVIII, Moon	O
8	Mabon	Animals	Elw	XVII, Star	I
9	Coel/Sul	Ecosystems	Cyswllt	XVI, Tower	W
10	Olwen	What is Present	Carchar	XV, Devil	E

Table 3: The paths of the Tree of Life

Number	To	From	Geomancy	Tarot	Coelbren
1	Ner	Naf	Pen y Ddraig	0, Fool	*, Bi
2	Byth	Naf	Ffordd	I, Magus	*, Ci
3	Byth	Ner	Merch	III, Empress	*, Ffi
4	Byw	Naf	Pobl	II, High Priestess	*, Di
5	Byw	Ner	Mab	IV, Emperor	*, Gi
6	Byw	Byth	Bendith Fach	VI, Lovers	*, Hi
7	Muner	Ner	Llosgwrn y Ddraig	V, Hierophant	*, Li
8	Muner	Byth	Coch	VII, Chariot	*, Mi
9	Muner	Byw	Gwyn	IX, Hermit	*, Ni
10	Modur	Byth	Tristwch	VIII, Strength	*, Pi
11	Modur	Muner	(see diagram)	XI, Justice	*, Ri
12	Ener	Byw	Llawenydd	X, Wheel of Fortune	*, Si
13	Ener	Muner	(see diagram)	XII, Hanged Man	*, Ti
14	Ener	Modur	(see diagram)	XIV, Temperance	*, Ddi
15	Dofydd	Muner	(see diagram)	4 Tens	*, Lli
16	Dofydd	Modur	(see diagram)	4 Nines	(unknown)
17	Perydd	Muner	(see diagram)	4 Sevens	*, Fi
18	Perydd	Ener	(see diagram)	4 Sixes	(unknown)
19	Perydd	Dofydd	(see diagram)	4 Fives	(unknown)
20	Celi	Muner	(see diagram)	XIII, Death	*, Chi
21	Celi	Dofydd	generation of Dyad	4 Threes	(unknown)
22	Celi	Perydd	generation of Monad	4 Twos	(unknown)

It is unnecessary to memorize these before practicing the *Litany of the Tree of Life*. Quite the contrary, regular practice of the *Litany of the Tree of Life* will assist in the process of memorizing these symbols for other uses.

A table of pronunciation of the Welsh words is included further back (see pp. 73–74).

Table 4: The names of the geomantic figures

Welsh name	Latin name	Welsh name	Latin name
Mab	Puer	Elw	Acquisitio
Colled	Amissio	Carchar	Carcer
Gwyn	Albus	Tristwch	Tristitia
Pobl	Populus	Llawenydd	Laetitia
Bendith Fawr	Fortuna Major	Llosgwrn y Ddraig	Cauda Draconis
Cyswllt	Conjunctio	Pen y Ddraig	Caput Draconis
Merch	Puella	Bendith Fach	Fortuna Minor
Coch	Rubeus	Ffordd	Via

INTRODUCTION TO THE LITANY

This litany is well suited for daily use as an alternative to the form of discursive meditation taught in the knowledge lectures of the Druidical Order of the Golden Dawn, and is specifically intended for the use of those who are engaged in intensive study of the Druidical Tree of Life. It may also be found suitable for practice on a more occasional basis, such as once per week, as a helpful addition to the regular meditations taught by the Order.

A litany such as this falls somewhere in the space between ritual and meditation. Like a meditation, it works primarily with consciousness rather than with the subtle energies directed in magic; like magic, it is in some sense a performance, in which performer and audience are one. Meditative attention on the symbols and concepts is important for the litany to have its proper effect, but so are the vocal and performative dimensions that give magic its power. Regular practice will teach each student to find a personally appropriate balance between these themes.

The extent to which ceremonial is used with this litany shall be left to the choice of each member of the Order. At minimum, a chair or a cushion for kneeling and a bell or chime for the knells will be sufficient for material preparation, and the litany may be used without other rituals. On the other hand, a temple may be opened in the Ovate Grade in full ceremonial form and the litany recited therein. Any desired point between these extremes may also be chosen; for example, incense may be burnt and candles lit during the recitation of the litany, without any other ceremony. Each practitioner should experiment and find the degree of ceremonial he finds appropriate to his needs.

The litany should be read aloud whenever circumstances permit. The recitation should be done as though reading aloud to an audience, clearly and somewhat slowly. The knells of the spheres, likewise, should not be rushed; the knell of each sphere is simply a series of strokes upon a bell or chime equal to the number of the sphere, thus, one for Celi, two for Perydd, and so forth. With practice, an appropriate pace for reading and knells will be found by each initiate.

Any given recitation of the litany traces out the route of one path upon the Tree of Life, invoking the beginning sphere, the ending sphere, and then the path connecting them. The paths are worked in a definite order, descending and then ascending, as given on the final pages of this book.

The attentive student will notice that in each case, all the paths that descend or ascend from a given sphere are worked sequentially before those appertaining to the next sphere in numerical order are begun. Thus, in the descending order, all three paths descending from Celi are worked in order, followed by the paths that descend from Perydd, and so on through the spheres. In the ascending order, in turn, all three paths ascending from Naf are worked, followed by the paths ascending from Ner, and so on.

Forty-eight recitations of the litany will be needed to complete the entire sequence, down from Celi to Naf and then back up to Celi; this will allow the whole sequence to be worked twice in a little over three months if practiced daily, or once in just under a year if practiced once a week. Either pattern of practice will be of considerable assistance to any person who seeks to attune himself or herself to the forces of the Druidical Tree of Life.

THE LITANY OF THE TREE OF LIFE
(The practitioner begins standing.)

Hu the Mighty, great Druid god, enlighten me through thy initiation.

In the light of the Golden Dawn and the presence of the holy powers of nature, I invoke the ten spheres of the Tree of Life. Celi the Hidden, the sphere of Being; Perydd the Cause, the sphere of Change; Dofydd the Tamer, the sphere of Rest; Ener the Namer, the sphere of Space; Modur the Mover, the sphere of Time; Muner the Lord, the sphere of Life; Byw the Living, the sphere of Fire; Byth the Eternal, the sphere of Air; Ner the Mighty, the sphere of Water; Naf the Shaper, the sphere of Earth.

Ten are the spheres and twenty-two the paths that constitute the Tree of Life, the grand symbol of the Mysteries. May they be brought into balance in the microcosm of myself as they are forever equilibrated in the macrocosm of the All.

> With this intent I awaken the path upon the Tree of Life that unites the spheres of … and …
>
> *(The practitioner sits or kneels. The knell of the beginning sphere is sounded.)*
>
> In the presence of the holy powers of nature, I invoke … the … th sphere.
>
> *(The invocation of the beginning sphere is recited.)*
>
> Powers of the … th sphere, may your blessing be upon my going forth.
>
> *(The knell of the ending sphere is sounded.)*

In the presence of the holy powers of nature, I invoke … the … th sphere.

(*The invocation of the ending sphere is recited.*)

Powers of the … th sphere, may your blessing be upon my coming in.

(*A single knell or knock is sounded.*)

Between the spheres of … and … the … th path wends its way. I invoke the powers of that path, that I may receive its blessing and radiate its light.

(*The invocation of the Path is recited; a period of silent meditation on the Path follows. When this is done, the practitioner stands and repeats the Universal Druid Prayer.*)*

Grant, O holy powers, thy protection;
  and in protection, strength;
  and in strength, understanding;
  and in understanding, knowledge;
  and in knowledge, the knowledge of justice;
  and in the knowledge of justice, the love of it;
  and in that love the love of all existences;
  and in the love of all existences, the love of Earth our mother and all goodness.

(*The following word is vibrated:*)

AWEN.

In the presence of the holy powers of nature, I thank and release the powers here invoked.

Hu the Mighty, great Druid god, enlighten me through thy initiation.

---

*Initiates of the Druid Grade of the DOGD may replace this prayer with the OIW Invocation if desired.

THE UNMANIFEST

Thou that art without name and without form, thou that art without qualities and without history, thou that art forever beyond the understanding of any created being, I invoke thee.

The Circle of Ceugant, the highest reality that can be imagined by the human mind, cannot contain thee. The primal point of Celi, the first reality that can be grasped by the human spirit, cannot express thee. All that I can know of thee is that I know thee not. Thou art the abyss of endless possibility, in which all abides that has not yet come into being.

Yet thou art also the source from which all things arise. Thou alone art reality; all else is appearance. Thou alone art stable; all else is a constant becoming and passing away. Thou art the strong dark earth that surrounds the roots of the Tree of Life, the first and final emptiness out of which arises all manifest existence.

Thou art the limitless realm of divinity that has not yet taken shape as deity. Thou art the unfathomable Ground of Being that has not yet given birth to nature. Thou art the cauldron of Annwn out of which individual existences have not yet been born. Where I am, thou art hidden, and where thou art I am not.

Infinite divinity beyond all my imaginings, may the powers of the Unmanifest be rightly disposed in my sphere of sensation. I pray that thou wilt guide me in the ways of thy Mysteries, that having arisen from the cauldron of Annwn through the circles of Abred, having been all things, known all things, and suffered all things, I may rise up rejoicing into the light of Gwynfydd.

(Note that in practical work with the Litany at those stages that deal with this text, the words marked "... the ... th sphere" and "the ... th sphere" are to be replaced simply by the words "the Unmanifest.")

CELI

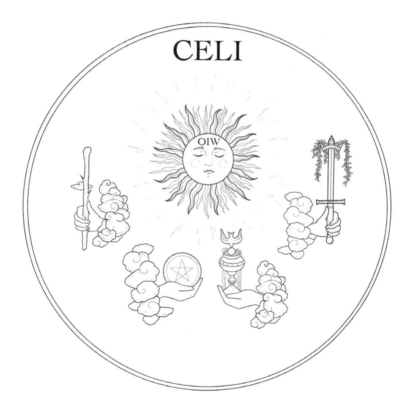

CELI, THE FIRST SPHERE

First point of light in the limitless beyond, source and sum of all things, whose name itself confesses the limits of my understanding, I invoke thee.

In the Circle of Ceugant, which no created being can traverse, thou art the ultimate reality toward which the human spirit can strive. Thou art the primal point, beyond space and time, being and becoming, force and form. In thee, all things are One Thing and there is no other.

The deity that dwells in thee abides in the ineffable, beyond knowledge and name. I affirm my ignorance of that mystery in the letters O, I, W.

In the world of nature, the glory of the sun shadows forth some part of the splendor of the first sphere. As all things on Earth draw being and life from the sun, may I always recall and reverence my source in thee.

Only the spark of inmost spirit in me, the essential flame that abides beyond time and change, may rightly aspire to reflect thine imperishable radiance. May that aspiration be fulfilled in time.

Taproot of the Tree of Life, that descendeth most deeply into the Unmanifest Ground of Being, thou art the undifferentiated wholeness out of which Monad and Dyad are generated; thou art shadowed forth by the four Aces in the Tarot; thou art one of the unknown letters of the primitive Coelbren, whose key is the Dasgubell Rodd.

Unknowable One whose name is veiled in the letters OIW, may the powers of the first sphere be rightly disposed in my sphere of sensation. I pray that thou wilt guide me in the ways of thy Mysteries, that having arisen from the cauldron of Annwn through the circles of Abred, having been all things, known all things, and suffered all things, I may rise up rejoicing into the light of Gwynfydd.

PERYDD, THE SECOND SPHERE

Second point of the creative Triad, being overflowing into becoming, origin of all power and all possibilities, I invoke thee.

In the Circle of Ceugant, which no created being can traverse, thou art the first reality the human spirit can name. Thou art the line of infinite extension, the power of the Dyad made manifest.

Hu the Mighty, the great Druid god, is the divinity that abides in thee, the herdsman of the stars and guide of the great journey, who causes darkness to dwell in its rightful place.

In the world of nature, the sun's outpouring radiance, which causes every change upon the Earth, expresses the power of the second sphere. As all things that live depend on the sunlight, so may I recognize my dependence on the power that brings all things into being.

The true and timeless will of the innermost spirit is thy manifestation in my microcosm. May every action I perform and every choice I make be in harmony with that true will.

Second great root of the Tree of Life, thou art the single point of fire made manifest; in the Tarot thou art shadowed forth by the four Fours; thou art one of the unknown letters of the primitive Coelbren, whose key is the Dasgubell Rodd.

Hu the Mighty, great Druid god, may the powers of the second sphere be rightly disposed in my sphere of sensation. I pray that thou wilt guide me in the ways of thy Mysteries, that having arisen from the cauldron of Annwn through the circles of Abred, having been all things, known all things, and suffered all things, I may rise up rejoicing into the light of Gwynfydd.

DOFYDD

DOFYDD, THE THIRD SPHERE

Third point and fulfillment of the creative Triad, becoming flowing ever back again into being, abiding presence beyond all change, I invoke thee.

In the Circle of Ceugant, which no created being can traverse, thou art the second reality the human spirit can name, standing forever equal with the first. Thou art the triangle of completion, expressing the power of the Triad; thou art the arc of the circle that returns forever to the point where it began.

Ced the Earth Mother is the divinity that abides in thee, the source of all life, the voyager upon the great deep, the eternal aid and helpmeet of every act of creation.

In the world of nature, the sun's enduring gravity, which holds the Earth in its orbit, expresses the power of the third sphere. As the Earth turns ever around the central sun, may I bend the circle of my life so that thou art its center.

The true and timeless understanding, the third aspect of the indwelling spirit, is thy manifestation in my microcosm. May my life and my thoughts be ever in harmony with that higher understanding.

Third great root of the Tree of Life, thou art the double point of fire made receptive and unmanifest; in the Tarot thou art shadowed forth by the four Eights; thou art one of the unknown letters of the primitive Coelbren, whose key is the Dasgubell Rodd.

Ced the Earth Mother, source of all Life, may the powers of the third sphere be rightly disposed in my sphere of sensation. I pray that thou wilt guide me in the ways of thy Mysteries, that having arisen from the cauldron of Annwn through the circles of Abred, having been all things, known all things, and suffered all things, I may rise up rejoicing into the light of Gwynfydd.

IAU

IAU, THE UNNUMBERED SPHERE

Unnumbered point between the supernal Triad and the septenary of creation, uniting and dividing the roots of the Tree of Life from its trunk and branches, I invoke thee.

Thou art the border of the Circle of Ceugant, to which every created being can aspire but which no created being can traverse. Thou art the spiral that unfolds from the union of line and circles, and reaches out from a central point to embrace all of being.

Ceridwen the Wise is the divinity that abides in thee, the keeper of the cauldron of the Mysteries, who gives the second birth to every initiate found worthy of wisdom.

In the world of nature the moon, which mediates between the heavens and the earth, expresses the power of the unnumbered sphere. As the moon waxes and wanes but ever reflects the sun, so through the changes of my life may I ever reflect the light of spirit.

The reflective consciousness which reaches from spirit to mind is thy manifestation in my microcosm. May I cultivate that consciousness, that I may attain Gwynfydd in this life.

Bole of the Tree of Life, where roots and branches join at the surface of the Ground of Being, thou art the double points of fire, air, and water made unmanifest; in the Tarot thou art shadowed forth by the sixteen court cards; thou art one of the unknown letters of the primitive Coelbren, whose key is the Dasgubell Rodd.

Ceridwen the Wise, keeper of the cauldron, may the powers of the unnumbered sphere be rightly disposed in my sphere of sensation. I pray that thou wilt guide me in the ways of thy Mysteries, that having arisen from the cauldron of Annwn through the circles of Abred, having been all things, known all things, and suffered all things, I may rise up rejoicing into the light of Gwynfydd.

ENER, THE FOURTH SPHERE

First manifestation outside the Ground of Being, principle of mercy and of greatness, source of all names and all individual existence, I invoke thee.

In the Circle of Gwynfydd thou art the highest of spheres, the summit of that to which created beings may aspire. Thou art the city of four gates and the quaternity of being, the Dyad reflected upon itself.

Belinus the Lord of the Heavens is the divinity that abides in thee, the archetype of kingship, whose wisdom holds the turning worlds in their courses.

In the world of nature, the material substances that compose the body of the Earth express the power of the fourth sphere. May I ever hold the elemental creation in reverence.

The power of intuition that guides the mind in the ways of wisdom is thy manifestation in my microcosm. May my intuition be well attuned to the Higher, and may I be ever attentive to its promptings.

First branch of the Tree of Life, thou art the single points of manifest fire and water joined by the double point of latent air; in the Tarot thou art the Trump named The World; thou art the last of the seven vowels of the Coelbren, the letter U.

Beli the Lord of Heaven, great shepherd of the stars, may the powers of the fourth sphere be rightly disposed in my sphere of sensation. I pray that thou wilt guide me in the ways of thy Mysteries, that having arisen from the cauldron of Annwn through the circles of Abred, having been all things, known all things, and suffered all things, I may rise up rejoicing into the light of Gwynfydd.

MODUR, THE FIFTH SPHERE

Second manifestation outside the Ground of Being, principle of severity and of change, source of all coming to being and passing away, I invoke thee.

In the Circle of Gwynfydd thou art the sphere of transformation and the door through which good and evil alike may enter. Thou art the five-pointed star of power, and through thee the Golden Section unfolds its hidden unity.

Taranis of the thunders is the divinity that abides in thee, the bull of the heavens, the master of the lightning flash.

In the world of nature, the cycles of time, greater and lesser, that bring all things into being and return them to the Unmanifest express the power of the fifth sphere. May I ever hold the cycles of creation in reverence.

The power of will that unites all the faculties of the self in orientation to purpose is thy manifestation in my microcosm. May my will be ever strong and single, and may it act in harmony with the great pattern of all things.

Second branch of the Tree of Life, thou art the single point of manifest air between the double points of latent fire and water; in the Tarot thou art the Trump named Judgment; thou art the sixth of the seven vowels of the Coelbren, the letter Y.

Taranis the Thunderer, great bull of the heavens, may the powers of the fifth sphere be rightly disposed in my sphere of sensation. I pray that thou wilt guide me in the ways of thy Mysteries, that having arisen from the cauldron of Annwn through the circles of Abred, having been all things, known all things, and suffered all things, I may rise up rejoicing into the light of Gwynfydd.

MUNER, THE SIXTH SPHERE

Third manifestation outside the Ground of Being, principle of harmony and of beauty, mighty power of balance at the mid-point of the Tree of Life, I invoke thee.

In the Circle of Gwynfydd thou art the sphere of initiation and redemption, the place of sacrifice where the lower is transmuted unto the higher. Thou art the vesica that unites the circles; thou art the star of six points, the double manifestation of the mystery of the Triad.

Hesus the Chief of Tree-Spirits is the divinity that abides in thee, he who sits in the first fork of the sacred oak, master of the green world and its wisdom.

In the world of nature, the miracle of life that reflects the macrocosm into countless microcosms expresses the power of the sixth sphere. May I be mindful that all things have died that I might live.

The power of thought by which the universe is presented and represented is thy manifestation in my microcosm. May my thoughts turn away from the false and unbalanced, that I may aspire ever toward the great symbols of wisdom and truth.

Strong trunk of the Tree of Life, thou art the figure Bendith Fawr, the power of the greater blessing; in the Tarot thou art the Trump named the Sun; thou art the first of the seven vowels of the Coelbren, the letter A.

Esus of the Oak, Chief of Tree-Spirits, may the powers of the sixth sphere be rightly disposed in my sphere of sensation. I pray that thou wilt guide me in the ways of thy Mysteries, that having arisen from the cauldron of Annwn through the circles of Abred, having been all things, known all things, and suffered all things, I may rise up rejoicing into the light of Gwynfydd.

BYW, THE SEVENTH SPHERE

Fourth manifestation outside the Ground of Being, great principle of love and of strife, highest reality known to the uninitiated soul, I invoke thee.

In the Circle of Abred thou art the sphere of Fire. Sevenfold are thy secrets; among the ten spheres thou art the virgin power that neither begets nor is begotten.

Elen of the Roads is the divinity that abides in thee, the spirit of dawn and dusk, the mistress of the old straight track and its Mysteries.

In the world of nature, the trees and herbs, and all other lives that draw their nourishment from the elements directly, express the power of the seventh sphere. May I ever hold the vegetable creation in reverence.

The power of feeling that unites all things in the everlasting dance of relationship is thy manifestation in my microcosm. May my emotions be forthright and free, and my heart open to every experience.

Third branch of the Tree of Life, thou art the figure Colled, the power of Loss; in the Tarot thou art the Trump named the Moon; thou art fourth of the seven vowels of the Coelbren, the letter O.

Elen of the Roads and the twilight, may the powers of the seventh sphere be rightly disposed in my sphere of sensation. I pray that thou wilt guide me in the ways of thy Mysteries, that having arisen from the cauldron of Annwn through the circles of Abred, having been all things, known all things, and suffered all things, I may rise up rejoicing into the light of Gwynfydd.

BYTH, THE EIGHTH SPHERE

Fifth manifestation outside the Ground of Being, principle of complexity and diversity, common ground of today's humanity, I invoke thee.

In the Circle of Abred thou art the sphere of Air. Thou art the eightfold star of power and the mystery of the quaternity doubled upon itself.

Mabon son of Modron, the child of light, is the divinity that abides in thee, the hidden one, the opener of the way.

In the world of nature, the animals, and all other lives that draw their nourishment from other living things, express the power of the eighth sphere. May I ever hold the animal creation in reverence.

The power of sense that perceives the universe is thy manifestation in my microcosm. May my senses be always keen and clear, and open to the wonder of the cosmos.

Fourth branch of the Tree of Life, thou art the figure Elw, the power of Gain; in the Tarot thou art the Trump named the Star; thou art the third of the seven vowels of the Coelbren, the letter I.

Mabon son of Modron, child of Light, may the powers of the eighth sphere be rightly disposed in my sphere of sensation. I pray that thou wilt guide me in the ways of thy Mysteries, that having arisen from the cauldron of Annwn through the circles of Abred, having been all things, known all things, and suffered all things, I may rise up rejoicing into the light of Gwynfydd.

NER, THE NINTH SPHERE

Sixth manifestation outside the Ground of Being, great treasure house of images and forms, common ground of all incarnate consciousness, I invoke thee.

In the Circle of Abred thou art the sphere of Water. Ninefold are thy Mysteries, the Triad made manifest in triple form.

Coel the woodland god and Sul the goddess of healing springs are the divinities that abide in thee, twofold as the Mysteries of generation are twofold.

In the world of nature, the dance of relationships that bind all living things together with one another and with the cosmos as a whole express the power of the ninth sphere. May I ever live in harmony with the balance of nature.

The etherial body and its sphere of sensation are thy manifestations in my microcosm. May life flow strongly through my subtle body and my sphere of sensation reflect clearly and truly the patterns of the macrocosm.

Fifth and midmost branch of the Tree of Life, thou art the figure Cyswllt, the power of Combination; in the Tarot thou art the Trump named the Tower; thou art the fifth of the seven vowels of the Coelbren, the letter W.

Coel and Sul, god and goddess of living nature, may the powers of the ninth sphere be rightly disposed in my sphere of sensation. I pray that thou wilt guide me in the ways of thy Mysteries, that having arisen from the cauldron of Annwn through the circles of Abred, having been all things, known all things, and suffered all things, I may rise up rejoicing into the light of Gwynfydd.

NAF, THE TENTH SPHERE

Seventh manifestation outside the Ground of Being, completion of the creative process, last and furthest of the spheres, I invoke thee.

In the Circle of Abred thou art the sphere of Earth. Tenfold art thou as the Tree is tenfold, the completed cycle returning unto the unity of Celi.

Olwen of the White Track is the divinity that abides in thee, the maiden of the springtime, child of the hawthorn giant.

In the world of nature, the actual phenomena of the living world in each moment and each place express the power of the tenth sphere. May I respect and reverence all that is.

The physical body in all its strengths and weaknesses is thy manifestation in my microcosm. May my body be blessed with health and with sufficient provision for all its needs.

Ultimate branch of the Tree of Life, thou art the figure Carchar, the power of Containment; in the Tarot thou art the Trump named the Devil; thou art the second of the seven vowels of the Coelbren, the letter E.

Olwen of the White Track, goddess of spring, may the powers of the tenth sphere be rightly disposed in my sphere of sensation. I pray that thou wilt guide me in the ways of thy Mysteries, that having arisen from the cauldron of Annwn through the circles of Abred, having been all things, known all things, and suffered all things, I may rise up rejoicing into the light of Gwynfydd.

NUMBERLESS PATH:
UNMANIFEST TO CELI

The Litany of the Tree of Life,
p. xvii.
The sphere readings:
   The Unmanifest, p. 1.
   Celi, the first sphere, p. 3.
The path reading:

First and final path of the Tree, that descends from the Unmanifest to form the first center of manifest reality and returns to the Unmanifest again, I invoke thee.

In thee there is not yet being or becoming, movement or stillness, time or space, darkness or light. The Three Rays that bring the universe into being arise after thee and depart before thee.

In thee the first seed of number, which will become Monad and Dyad, lies unawakened. Thou art that which comes before the first card of the Tarot and the first letter of the Coelbren.

As the hidden One we name OIW emerges from the unseen and unknowable, as the sun emerges out of interstellar space, so may I unite in myself the powers of the Unmanifest and Celi, that I may accomplish the work of the Mysteries now and always.

CELI

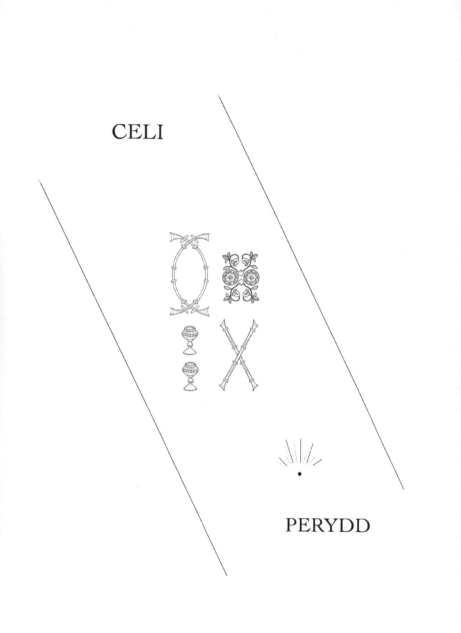

PERYDD

TWENTY-SECOND PATH: CELI TO PERYDD

The Litany of the Tree of Life, p. xvii.

The sphere readings:

   Celi, the first sphere, p. 3.

   Perydd, the second sphere, p. 5.

The path reading:

Path of the first creative influx, that unites the sphere of pure being with the sphere of pure becoming, I invoke thee.

Thou art the springing-forth of the Ray of Power at the right hand of the Three Rays of Light. From thee comes forth radiance that descends to the uttermost part of the Tree.

Thou art the generation of the Monad. In the Tarot thou art shadowed forth by the four Twos. Thou art one of the unknown letters of the primitive Coelbren, whose key is the Dasgubell Rodd.

As Hu the Mighty reveals that hidden One we name OIW, as the sun is united with its rays, so may I unite in myself the powers of Celi and Perydd, that I may accomplish the work of the Mysteries now and always.

CELI

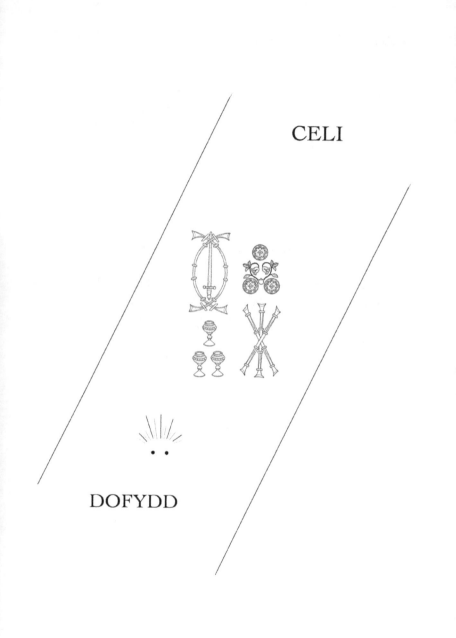

DOFYDD

TWENTY-FIRST PATH: CELI TO DOFYDD

The Litany of the Tree of Life,
p. xvii.
The sphere readings:
   Celi, the first sphere, p. 3.
   Dofydd, the third sphere,
p. 7.
The path reading:

Path of perfection that unites the beginning of the creative process with its end, I invoke thee.

Thou art the first springing-forth of the Ray of Knowledge at the left hand of the Three Rays of Light. From thee comes forth radiance that descends to the uttermost parts of the Tree.

Thou art the generation of the Dyad. In the Tarot thou art shadowed forth by the four Threes. Thou art one of the unknown letters of the primitive Coelbren, whose key is the Dasgubell Rodd.

As Ced the Earth Mother brings into manifestation that hidden One we name OIW, as the sun is united with its gravity, so may I unite in myself the powers of Celi and Dofydd, that I may accomplish the work of the Mysteries now and always.

CELI

MUNER

TWENTIETH PATH, UPPER HALF: CELI TO IAU

The Litany of the Tree of Life, p. xvii.

The sphere readings:

    Celi, the first sphere, p. 3.

    Iau, the unnumbered sphere, p. 9.

The Path Reading:

Path of involution by which the transcendent reality descends into manifestation, I invoke thee.

Thou art the first springing-forth of the Ray of Peace, the middlemost of the Three Rays. From thee comes forth radiance that descends to the uttermost part of the Tree.

Thou art the double point of latent fire united with the single point of manifest air. In the Tarot thou art the Trump named Death. Thou art one of the unknown letters of the primitive Coelbren, whose key is the Dasgubell Rodd.

As the cauldron of Ceridwen makes manifest the power of that hidden one we name OIW, as all created existence turns toward the Sun, so may I unite in myself the powers of Celi and Iau, that I may accomplish the work of the Mysteries now and always.

CELI

MUNER

TWENTIETH PATH, LOWER HALF: IAU TO MUNER

The Litany of the Tree of Life, p. xvii.

The sphere readings:

Iau, the unnumbered sphere, p. 9.

Muner, the sixth sphere, p. 15.

The path reading:

Path of exaltation by which all that is immanent in manifestation returns to the transcendent, I invoke thee.

Thou art the completion of the first path upon the Ray of Peace. Thou art one among the seven vertical paths of the Tree, by which the polarities of being are brought into full expression.

Thou art the double point of latent fire united with the single point of manifest air. In the Tarot thou art the Trump named Death. Thou art the letter Chi of the Coelbren.

As Hesus the Chief of Tree-Spirits draws on the healing powers of the cauldron of Ceridwen, as all created existences return to the Unmanifest, so may I unite in myself the powers of Iau and Muner, that I may accomplish the work of the Mysteries now and always.

PERYDD  ∴ DOFYDD

NINETEENTH PATH: PERYDD TO DOFYDD

The Litany of the Tree of Life, p. xvii.

The sphere readings:

  Perydd, the second sphere, p. 5.

  Dofydd, the third sphere, p. 7.

The path reading:

Path of paradox that unites the two primal powers of the Ground of Being, I invoke thee.

Thou bringest into harmony the Ray of Power with the Ray of Knowledge. Thou art one of the three reciprocal paths of the Tree, by which the polarities of being are held in balance.

Thou art the single point of manifested fire combined with the double point of latent air. In the Tarot thou art shadowed forth by the four Fives. Thou art one of the unknown letters of the primitive Coelbren, whose key is the Dasgubell Rodd.

As Hu the Mighty unites with Ced the Earth Mother, as the radiance and gravity of the Sun shape all things on Earth, so may I unite in myself the powers of Perydd and Dofydd, that I may accomplish the work of the Mysteries now and always.

PERYDD

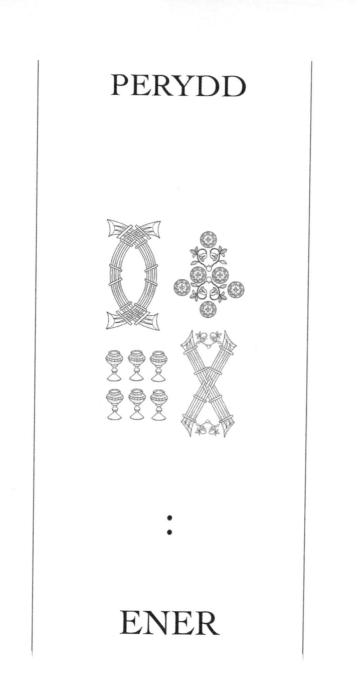

:

ENER

EIGHTEENTH PATH: PERYDD TO ENER

The Litany of the Tree of Life,
p. xvii.
The sphere readings:
Perydd, the second sphere,
p. 5.
Ener, the fourth sphere,
p. 11.
The path reading:

Path of creation by which light descends into the realm of manifestation, I invoke thee.

Thou art the second path upon the Ray of Power. Thou art one among the seven vertical paths of the Tree, by which the polarities of being are brought into full expression.

Thou art the single points of manifested fire and air. Thou art shadowed forth by the four Sixes of the Tarot. Thou art one of the unknown letters of the primitive Coelbren, whose key is the Dasgubell Rodd.

As Hu the Mighty places the crown upon the brow of Belinus, as the Sun's radiance warms the substance of the Earth, so may I unite in myself the powers of Perydd and Ener, that I may accomplish the work of the Mysteries now and always.

PERYDD

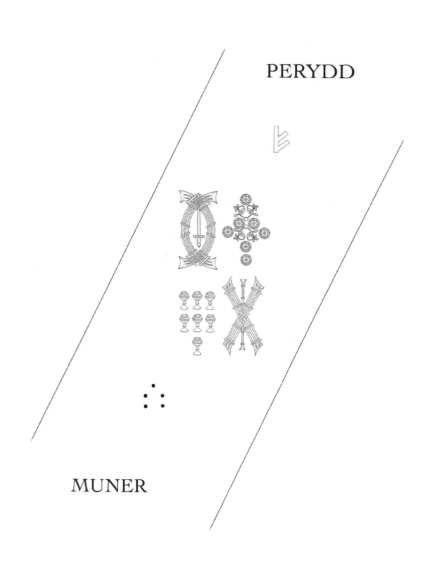

MUNER

SEVENTEENTH PATH: PERYDD TO MUNER

The Litany of the Tree of Life,
p. xvii.
The sphere readings:
Perydd, the second sphere,
p. 5.
Muner, the sixth sphere,
p. 15.
The path reading:

Path of radiance by which the heart of the Tree is kindled into light, I invoke thee.

Thou descendest from the sphere of highest power to the sphere of greatest harmony. Thou art one among the twelve diagonal paths of the Tree, by which the polarities of being are woven into unity.

Thou art the single point of manifest fire with the double points of latent air and water. In the Tarot thou art shadowed forth by the four Sevens. Thou art the letter Fi of the Coelbren.

As Hu the Mighty is made manifest through Esus Chief of Tree-Spirits, as the Sun's radiance kindles life on Earth, so may I unite in myself the powers of Perydd and Muner, that I may accomplish the work of the Mysteries now and always.

DOFYDD

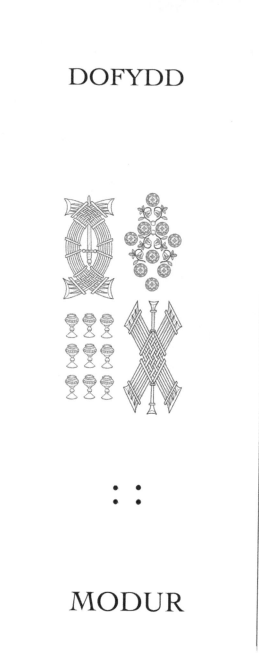

MODUR

SIXTEENTH PATH: DOFYDD TO MODUR

The Litany of the Tree of Life, p. xvii.
The sphere readings:
    Dofydd, the third sphere, p. 7.
    Modur, the Fifth Sphere, p. 13.
The path reading:

Path of stillness by which the realm of change comes to rest in the eternal, I invoke thee.

Thou art the second path upon the Ray of Knowledge. Thou art one among the seven vertical paths of the Tree, by which the polarities of being are brought into full expression.

Thou art the double point of latent fire combined with the double point of latent air. Thou art shadowed forth by the four Nines of the Tarot. Thou art one of the unknown letters of the primitive Coelbren, whose key is the Dasgubell Rodd.

As Ced the Earth Mother gives birth to the mighty Bull of Heaven, as the Sun's gravity governs the cycle of the seasons, so may I unite in myself the powers of Dofydd and Modur, that I may accomplish the work of the Mysteries now and always.

DOFYDD

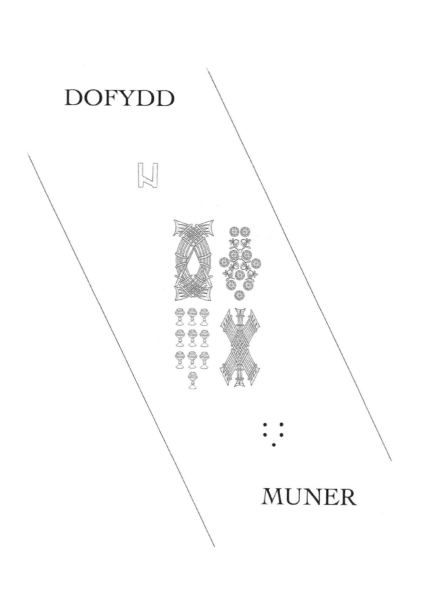

MUNER

FIFTEENTH PATH: DOFYDD TO MUNER

The Litany of the Tree of Life, p. xvii.

The sphere readings:

Dofydd, the third sphere, p. 7.

Muner, the sixth sphere, p. 15.

The path reading:

Path of finality by which life returns to the eternal and unchanging, I invoke thee.

Thou descendest from the sphere of greatest peace to the sphere of greatest harmony. Thou art one among the twelve diagonal paths of the Tree, by which the polarities of being are woven into unity.

Thou art the double points of latent fire and air combined with the single point of manifested water. In the Tarot thou art shadowed forth by the four Tens. Thou art the letter Lli of the Coelbren.

As Ced the Earth Mother fosters Hesus the Chief of Tree-Spirits, as the power of gravity guides living things in their growth, so may I unite in myself the powers of Dofydd and Muner, that I may accomplish the work of the Mysteries now and always.

ENER  : MODUR

FOURTEENTH PATH: ENER TO MODUR

The Litany of the Tree of Life,
p. xvii.
The sphere readings:
    Ener, the fourth sphere,
p. 11.
    Modur, the fifth sphere,
p. 13.
The path reading:

Path of balance by which the Rays of Power and Knowledge are equilibrated, I invoke thee.

Thou holdest in perfect equipoise the two great pillars of the Tree. Thou art one of the three reciprocal paths of the Tree, by which the polarities of being are held in balance.

Thou art the single points of manifested fire, air, and water. In the Tarot thou art the Trump named Temperance. Thou art the letter Ddi of the Coelbren.

As Belinus the great king is the brother of Taranis the Thunderer, as the cycles of nature transform and renew the substances of the Earth, so may I unite in myself the powers of Ener and Modur, that I may accomplish the work of the Mysteries now and always.

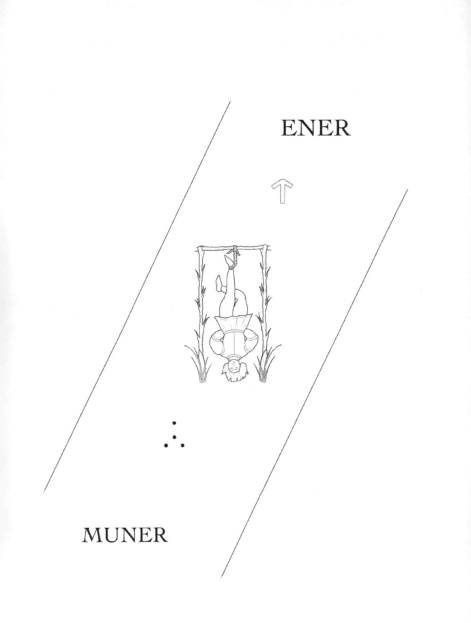

ENER

MUNER

THIRTEENTH PATH: ENER TO MUNER

The Litany of the Tree of Life,
p. xvii.
The sphere readings:
    Ener, the fourth sphere,
p. 11.
    Muner, the sixth sphere,
p. 15.
The path reading:

Path of sacrifice by which the macrocosm directs the forces of life, I invoke thee.

Thou descendest from the sphere of Space to the sphere of Life. Thou art one among the twelve diagonal paths of the Tree, by which the polarities of being are woven into unity.

Thou art the single points of manifested fire and air combined with the double point of latent water. In the Tarot thou art the Trump named the Hanged Man. Thou art the letter Ti of the Coelbren.

As Belinus the great king grants his protection to Hesus Chief of Tree-Spirits, as the substances of the Earth are the foundations of life, so may I unite in myself the powers of Ener and Muner, that I may accomplish the work of the Mysteries now and always.

ENER

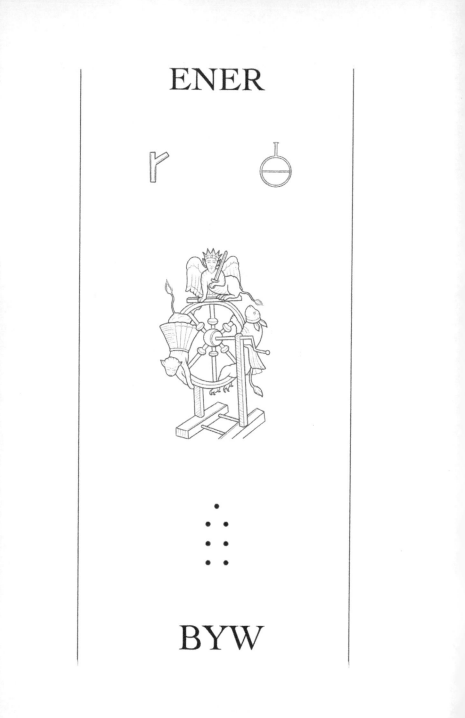

BYW

TWELFTH PATH: ENER TO BYW

The Litany of the Tree of Life, p. xvii.

The sphere readings:

Ener, the fourth sphere, p. 11.

Byw, the seventh sphere, p. 17.

The path reading:

Path of destiny by which the macrocosm protects and nourishes the vegetable creation, I invoke thee.

Thou descendest from the sphere of Space to the sphere of Fire. Thou art one among the seven vertical paths of the Tree, by which the polarities of being are brought into full expression.

Thou art the figure Llawenydd, the power of Ascent. In the Tarot thou art the Trump named the Wheel of Fortune. Thou art the letter Si of the Coelbren.

As Belinus the great king blesses his daughter Elen of the Roads, as the substances of the Earth support the green things growing upon them, so may I unite in myself the powers of Ener and Byw, that I may accomplish the work of the Mysteries now and always.

MODUR

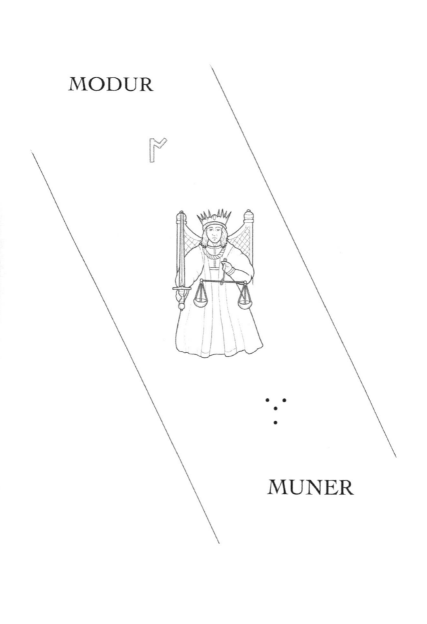

MUNER

ELEVENTH PATH: MODUR TO MUNER

The Litany of the Tree of Life,
p. xvii.
The sphere readings:
 Modur, the fifth sphere,
p. 13.
 Muner, the sixth sphere,
p. 15.
The path reading:

Path of justice by which the macrocosm gives form to the manifestations of life, I invoke thee.

Thou descendest from the sphere of Time to the sphere of Life. Thou art among the twelve diagonal paths of the Tree, by which the polarities of being are woven into unity.

Thou art the double point of latent fire combined with the single points of manifest air and water. In the Tarot thou art the Trump named Justice. Thou art the letter Ri of the Coelbren.

As Taranis the Thunderer sends the lightning to Hesus Chief of Tree-Spirits, as the cycles of the seasons give rhythm to life, so may I unite in myself the powers of Modur and Muner, that I may accomplish the work of the Mysteries now and always.

MODUR

BYTH

TENTH PATH: MODUR TO BYTH

The Litany of the Tree of Life, p. xvii.
The sphere readings:
   Modur, the fifth sphere, p. 13.
   Byth, the eighth sphere, p. 19.
The path reading:

Path of power by which the macrocosm protects and nourishes the animal creation, I invoke thee.

Thou descendest from the sphere of Time to the sphere of Air. Thou art one among the seven vertical paths of the Tree, by which the polarities of being are brought into full expression.

Thou art the figure Tristwch, the power of Descent. In the Tarot thou art the Trump named Strength. Thou art the letter Pi of the Coelbren.

As Taranis the Thunderer blesses Mabon the child of light, as the cycles of the seasons guide the animal creation in its ways, so may I unite in myself the powers of Modur and Byth, that I may accomplish the work of the Mysteries now and always.

MUNER

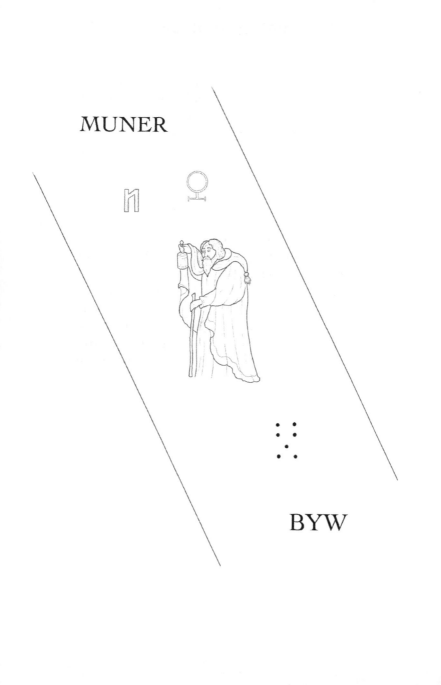

BYW

NINTH PATH: MUNER TO BYW

The Litany of the Tree of Life,
p. xvii.
The sphere readings:
   Muner, the sixth sphere,
p. 15.
   Byw, the seventh sphere,
p. 17.
The path reading:

Path of contemplation by which life flows into the vegetable creation, I invoke thee.

Thou descendest from the sphere of Life to the sphere of Fire. Thou art among the twelve diagonal paths of the Tree, by which the polarities of being are woven into unity.

Thou art the figure Gwyn, the power of Peace. In the Tarot thou art the Trump named the Hermit. Thou art the letter Ni of the Coelbren.

As Hesus Chief of Tree-Spirits rejoices in the dance of Elen of the Roads, as life is made manifest in the vegetable creation, so may I unite in myself the powers of Muner and Byw that I may accomplish the work of the Mysteries now and always.

MUNER

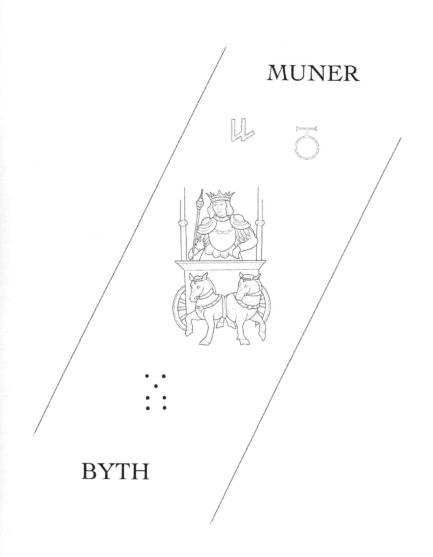

BYTH

EIGHTH PATH: MUNER TO BYTH

The Litany of the Tree of Life,
p. xvii.
The sphere readings:
Muner, the sixth sphere,
p. 15.
Byth, the eighth sphere,
p. 19.
The path reading:

Path of triumph by which life flows into the animal creation, I invoke thee.

Thou descendest from the sphere of Life to the sphere of Air. Thou art one among the twelve diagonal paths of the Tree, by which the polarities of being are woven into unity.

Thou art the figure Coch, the power of Passion. In the Tarot thou art the Trump named the Chariot. Thou art the letter Mi of the Coelbren.

As Hesus Chief of Tree-Spirits rejoices in the play of Mabon the child of light, as life is made manifest in the animal creation, so may I unite in myself the powers of Muner and Byth, that I may accomplish the work of the Mysteries now and always.

MUNER

NER

SEVENTH PATH: MUNER TO NER

The Litany of the Tree of Life,
p. xvii.
The sphere readings:
    Muner, the sixth sphere,
p. 15.
    Ner, the ninth sphere,
p. 21.
The path reading:

Path of initiation by which life flows into nature's web of relationships, I invoke thee.

Thou descendest from the sphere of Life to the sphere of Water. Thou art one among the seven vertical paths of the Tree, by which the polarities of being are brought into full expression.

Thou art the figure Llosgwrn y Ddraig, the power of completion. In the Tarot thou art the Trump named the Hierophant. Thou art the letter Li of the Coelbren.

As Hesus Chief of Tree-Spirits unites with Coel and Sul in the work of healing, as life is manifest in the relationships of the living, so may I unite in myself the powers of Muner and Ner, that I may accomplish the work of the Mysteries now and always.

BYW :·: BYTH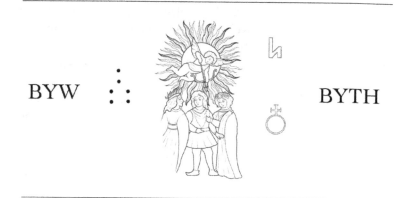

SIXTH PATH: BYW TO BYTH

The Litany of the Tree of Life,
p. xvii.
The sphere readings:
   Byw, the seventh sphere,
p. 17.
   Byth, the eighth sphere,
p. 19.
The path reading:

Path of union by which the Rays of Power and Knowledge unite in manifestation, I invoke thee.

Thou holdest in harmony the bases of the two great pillars of the Tree. Thou art one of the three reciprocal paths of the Tree, by which the polarities of being are held in balance.

Thou art the figure Bendith Fach, the power of the lesser blessing. In the Tarot thou art the Trump named the Lovers. Thou art the letter Hi of the Coelbren.

As Elen of the Roads shows the way to the hidden Mabon, as the animal and vegetable creation weave together the world of nature, so may I unite in myself the powers of Byth and Byw, that I may accomplish the work of the Mysteries now and always.

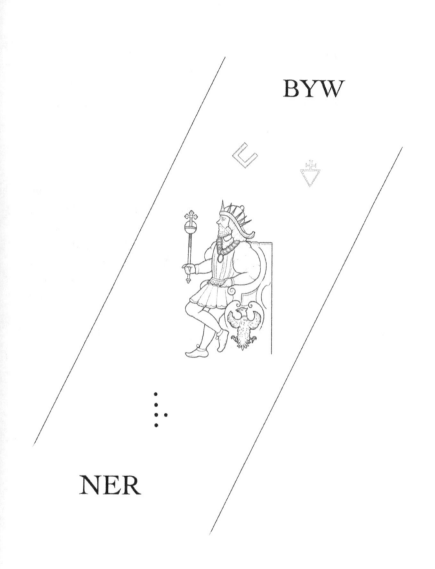

FIFTH PATH: BYW TO NER

The Litany of the Tree of Life,
p. xvii.
The sphere readings:
   Byw, the seventh sphere,
p. 17.
   Ner, the ninth sphere,
p. 21.
The path reading:

Path of dominion by which force expresses itself in nature, I invoke thee.

Thou descendest from the sphere of Fire to the sphere of Water. Thou art one among the twelve diagonal paths of the Tree, by which the polarities of being are woven into unity.

Thou art the figure Mab, the power of the Masculine. In the Tarot thou art the Trump named the Emperor. Thou art the letter Gi of the Coelbren.

As Elen opens the way to Coel and Sul, as the vegetable creation weaves itself into the patterns of nature, so may I unite in myself the powers of Byw and Ner, that I may accomplish the work of the Mysteries now and always.

BYW

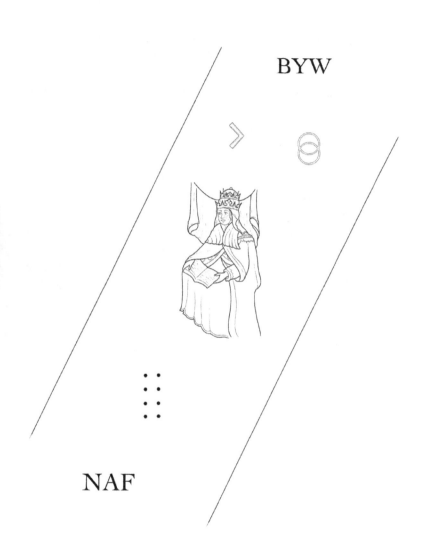

NAF

FOURTH PATH: BYW TO NAF

The Litany of the Tree of Life,
p. xvii.
The sphere readings:
Byw, the seventh sphere,
p. 17.
Naf, the tenth sphere,
p. 23.
The Path Reading:

Path of wisdom by which force descends into the world of matter, I invoke thee.

Thou art the last path upon the Ray of Power, descending from the sphere of Fire to the sphere of Earth. Through thee the right hand current that flows from Celi reaches its fulfillment.

Thou art the figure Pobl, the power of the Many. In the Tarot thou art the Trump named the High Priestess. Thou art the letter Di of the Coelbren.

As Elen of the Roads makes clear the way to Olwen of the White Track, as the vegetable creation helps shape the world of matter, so may I unite in myself the powers of Byw and Naf, that I may accomplish the work of the Mysteries now and always.

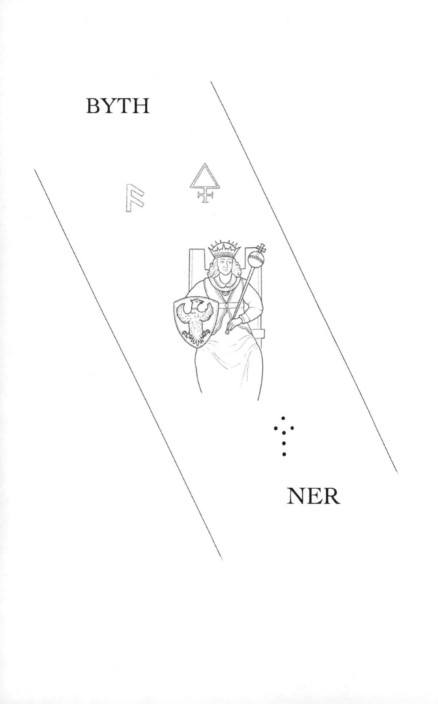

THIRD PATH: BYTH TO NER

The Litany of the Tree of Life, p. xvii.

The sphere readings:

   Byth, the eighth sphere, p. 19.

   Ner, the ninth sphere, p. 21.

The path reading:

Path of abundance by which form expresses itself in nature, I invoke thee.

Thou descendest from the sphere of Air to the sphere of Water. Thou art one among the twelve diagonal paths of the Tree, by which the polarities of being are woven together into unity.

Thou art the figure Merch, the power of the Feminine. In the Tarot thou art the Trump named the Empress. Thou art the letter Ffi of the Coelbren.

As Mabon the child of light is revealed through Coel and Sul, as the animal creation weaves itself into the patterns of nature, so may I unite in myself the powers of Byth and Ner, that I may accomplish the work of the Mysteries now and always.

BYTH

NAF

SECOND PATH: BYTH TO NAF

The Litany of the Tree of Life,
p. xvii.

The sphere readings:

Byth, the eighth sphere,
p. 19.

Naf, the tenth sphere,
p. 23.

The path reading:

Path of mastery by which form descends into the world of matter, I invoke thee.

Thou art the last path upon the Ray of Knowledge, descending from the sphere of Air to the sphere of Earth. Through thee the left hand current that flows from Celi reaches its fulfillment.

Thou art the figure Ffordd, the power of Solitude. In the Tarot thou art the Trump named the Magician. Thou art the letter Ci of the Coelbren.

As Mabon the child of light opens the way to Olwen of the White Track, as the animal creation helps shape the world of matter, so may I unite in myself the powers of Byth and Naf, that I may accomplish the work of the Mysteries now and always.

NER

NAF

FIRST PATH: NER TO NAF

The Litany of the Tree of Life, p. xvii.
The sphere readings:
Ner, the ninth sphere, p. 21.
Naf, the tenth sphere, p. 23.
The path reading:

Path of experience by which nature governs the world of matter, I invoke thee.

Thou art the last path upon the Ray of Peace, descending from the sphere of Water to the sphere of Earth. Through thee the central current that flows from Celi reaches its fulfillment.

Thou art the figure Pen y Ddraig, the power of Beginning. In the Tarot thou art the Trump named the Fool. Thou art the letter Bi of the Coelbren.

As Coel and Sul bless Olwen of the White Track, as the laws of nature govern the phenomena thereof, so may I unite in myself the powers of Ner and Naf, that I may accomplish the work of the Mysteries now and always.

PRONUNCIATION OF WELSH TERMS

(Note that when "th" is underlined it is voiced, as in "these clothes," not voiceless as in "thin broth." Ll is a sound not found in English and is best learned by listening to recordings of Welsh speakers; it is indicated here by the letters "lh.")

Abred—AH-bred
Annwn—ANN-oon
Beli—BEL-ee
Belinus—BEL-in-us
Bendith—BEN-dith
Byth—BITH
Byw—BEE-oo
Carchar—KAR-khar
Ced—KEHD
Celi—KEH-lee
Ceugant—KYE-gant
Coch—KOKH
Coel—CO-ul
Coelbren—CO-ul-bren
Colled—COLH-ed
Cyswllt—CUS-oolht
Dasgubell—DAS-gi-belh
Ddraig—THRAYG
Dofydd—DOH-vuth
Elen—ELL-en
Elw—ELL-oo
Ener—EN-er
Esus—ES-is

Fach—FAKH
Fawr—FAH-oor
Ffordd—FOR<u>TH</u>
Gwyn—GWIN
Gwynfydd—GWIN-vu<u>th</u>
Hesus—HEH-sis
Hu—HE
Llawenydd—LHA-wen-u<u>th</u>
Llosgwrn—LHOS-goorn
Mab—MAHB
Mabon—MAH-bon
Merch—MERKH
Modur—MOH-dir
Muner—MIH-ner
Naf—NAHV
Ner—NEHR
Olwen—OL-wen
Pen—PEN
Perydd—PER-u<u>th</u>
Pobl—POB-l
Rodd—RO<u>TH</u>
Sul—SIL
Taranis—TAR-an-is
y—uh

THE DESCENDING ORDER

1. unmanifest—sphere 1, Celi—Unnumbered path
2. sphere 1, Celi—sphere 2, Perydd—22nd path
3. sphere 1, Celi—sphere 3, Dofydd—21st path
4. sphere 1, Celi—unnumbered sphere, Iau—20th path
5. sphere 2, Perydd—sphere 3, Dofydd—19th path
6. sphere 2, Perydd—sphere 4, Ener—18th path
7. sphere 2, Perydd—sphere 6, Muner—17th path
8. sphere 3, Dofydd—sphere 5, Modur—16th path
9. sphere 3, Dofydd—sphere 6, Muner—15th path
10. unnumbered sphere, Iau—sphere 6, Muner—20th path
11. sphere 4, Ener—sphere 5, Modur—14th path
12. sphere 4, Ener—sphere 6, Muner—13th path
13. sphere 4, Ener—sphere 7, Byw—12th path
14. sphere 5, Modur—sphere 6, Muner—11th path
15. sphere 5, Modur—sphere 8, Byth—10th path
16. sphere 6, Muner—sphere 7, Byw—9th path
17. sphere 6, Muner—sphere 8, Byth—8th path
18. sphere 6, Muner—sphere 9, Ner—7th path
19. sphere 7, Byw—sphere 8, Byth—6th path
20. sphere 7, Byw—sphere 9, Ner—5th path
21. sphere 7, Byw—sphere 10, Naf—4th path
22. sphere 8, Byth—sphere 9, Ner—3rd path
23. sphere 8, Byth—sphere 10, Naf—2nd path
24. sphere 9, Ner—sphere 10, Naf—1st Path

THE ASCENDING ORDER

1. Sphere 10, Naf—Sphere 9, Ner—1st path
2. Sphere 10, Naf—Sphere 8, Byth—2nd path
3. Sphere 10, Naf—Sphere 7, Byw—4th path
4. Sphere 9, Ner—Sphere 8, Byth—3rd path
5. Sphere 9, Ner—Sphere 7, Byw—5th path
6. Sphere 9, Ner—Sphere 6, Muner—7th path
7. Sphere 8, Byth—Sphere 7, Byw—6th path
8. Sphere 8, Byth—Sphere 6, Muner—8th path
9. Sphere 8, Byth—Sphere 5, Modur—10th path
10. Sphere 7, Byw—Sphere 6, Muner—9th path
11. Sphere 7, Byw—Sphere 4, Ener—12th path
12. Sphere 6, Muner—Sphere 5, Modur—11th path
13. Sphere 6, Muner—Sphere 4, Ener—13th path
14. Sphere 6, Muner—Sphere 3, Dofydd—15th path
15. Sphere 6, Muner—Sphere 2, Perydd—17th path
16. Sphere 6, Muner—Unnumbered Sphere, Iau—20th path
17. Sphere 5, Modur—Sphere 4, Ener—14th path
18. Sphere 5, Modur—Sphere 3, Dofydd—16th path
19. Sphere 4, Ener—Sphere 2, Perydd—18th path
20. Sphere 3, Dofydd—Sphere 2, Perydd—19th path
21. Unnumbered Sphere, Iau—Sphere 1, Celi—20th path
22. Sphere 3, Dofydd—Sphere 1, Celi—21st path
23. Sphere 2, Perydd—Sphere 1, Celi—22nd path
24. Sphere 1, Celi—Unmanifest—Unnumbered Path

BIBLIOGRAPHY

Carr-Gomm, Philip, *In the Grove of the Druids: The Druid Teachings of Ross Nichols* (London: Watkins, 2002).

Chadwick, Nora, *The Druids* (Cardiff, UK: University of Wales Press, 1966).

Gray, William, *The Office of the Holy Tree of Life* (Dallas, TX: Sangreal Foundation, 1970).

Gray, William, *Sangreal Ceremonies and Rituals* (York Beach, MT: Weiser, 1986).

Greer, John Michael, *The Celtic Golden Dawn* (Woodbury, MN: Llewellyn Worldwide, 2013).

Greer, John Michael, *The Coelbren Alphabet* (Woodbury, MN: Llewellyn Worldwide, 2017).

Greer, John Michael, *The Mysteries of Merlin* (Woodbury, MN: Llewellyn Worldwide, 2020).

Richardson, Alan, and Geoff Hughes, *Ancient Magicks for a New Age* (St. Paul, MN: Llewellyn Publications, 1992).

Scholem, Gershom, *The Origins of the Kabbalah* (Princeton, NJ: Princeton University Press, 1990).